TULUM ON A BUDGET

Local Secrets To Save You Thousands, Avoid Newbie Mistakes & Have An Incredible Time!
ALLY CAVOSIE

TULUM
A BUDGET

Local Secrets To Save Thousands, Avoid Newbie Mistakes

&

Have The Best Time In Tulum!

By

Ally Cavosie

Inside out Traveler
Copyright © 2022 by Ally Cavosie.

For information contact :
www.TheGirlGang.Co

First Edition: May 2022

ABOUT AUTHOR

Ally Cavosie is passionate about helping people connect deeply with themselves and others. She was ready to see the world and what it offered, so she quit her corporate job in 2018 and never looked back. She was sick of mundane life and decided to redesign her whole life.

After traveling to 13+ countries in a year and a half and 23+ countries total, she settled down in Tulum, Mexico, in July 2020 to plant roots and build a community to support local ex-pats.

She Created the Tulum Girl Gang after three weeks of being in Tulum, and since its inception, The Girl Gang grew to over 7,000 members in just a little over a year and a half. The group redefines the way women come together to create powerful change in the world, and she supports women in feeling supported, safe, and connected in Tulum.

She's a yogi, a health lover, a coach, a mentor, a friend, a traveler, and a creative mind. After living in Tulum for almost two years, she decided to write down everything she's learned living here since most people experience a huge learning curve upon arriving. She has become a go-to resource for many in Tulum.

She is also the Author of Insideout Traveler: Get Unstuck Find Alignment & Start Traveling The World.

She believes in the law of reciprocity, trusting the universe has her back every step of the way. She lives to experience and learn. Her hope is that this book supports you in learning as much as possible to have the most beautiful experience in Tulum.

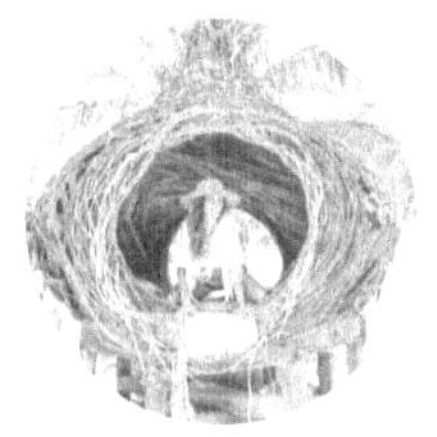

FIND ME

Email :
Alyssac@Live.com

Website :
www.TheGirlGang.Co

Instagram :
@Insideout.Traveler

WhatsApp:
+1.518.229.9283

CONTENTS

Chapter 5: **Where To In Tulum** 102

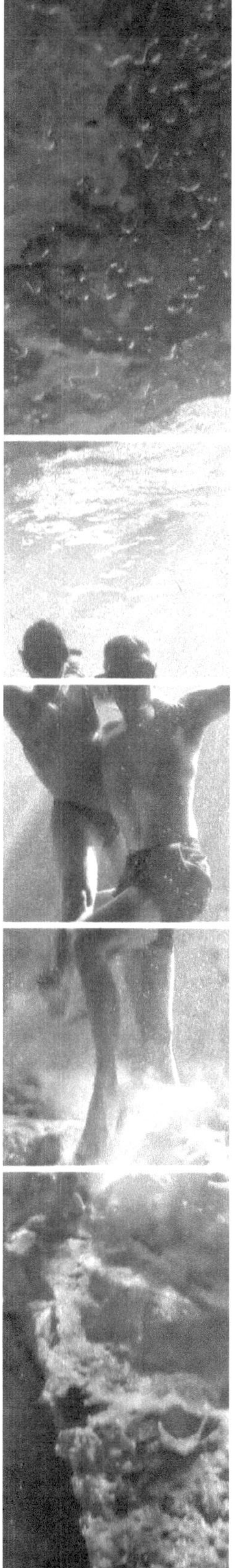

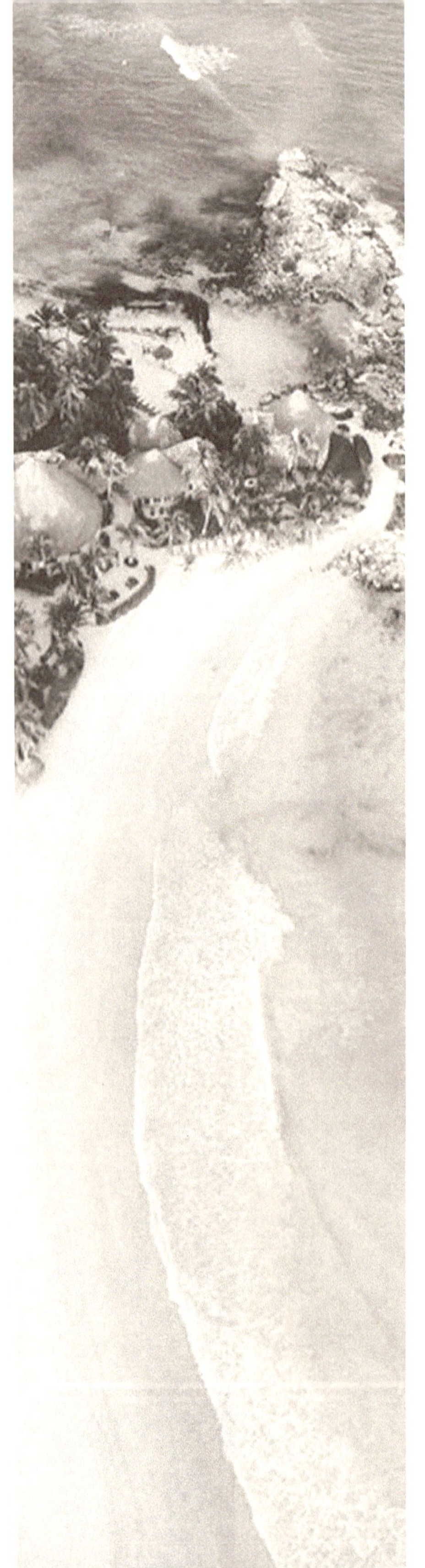

Intro

My name is Ally Cavosie. I quit my corporate job almost five years ago to travel the world. I knew more was out there, and I was determined to find it. After living out of a backpack for a year and a half, I was craving roots and community, so I settled down in a vibrant little town called Tulum, Mexico, in July 2020. After three days in Tulum, I knew that 'more' that I was looking for was here, and I never looked back. Living in Tulum for the last two years has taught me so much. It's been an experience of a lifetime, and I am so excited to share this beautiful town with you. I've learned the ins and outs of everything you need to know to have a successful experience in Tulum.

The thing about Tulum is that you can experience many

curveballs. It can be turbulent for some if you aren't prepared. Many of the norms you experience in Tulum are not the same as in first-world countries. Things that are easy in home countries can sometimes be hard here.

That's what inspired this book! I have done all the research and all the heavy lifting for you. I've been running several informative WhatsApp chats in Tulum for almost two years, so I've constantly learned new things every day. Not to mention experiencing all of my own experiences! I've made all the mistakes, so you don't have to. When a problem arises, just pull out this guide to get reliable and accurate information to support you while staying in Tulum.

Tulum is also a tourist destination, and because of this, it is so easy to get ripped off. So, if you look like a tourist, don't have an understanding of the place, or don't speak Spanish, it's easy to get taken advantage of. You could pay $5 for an ice cream cone or $1. You could pay $50 for a massage or $300. Would that make this book worth it if you can get the best quality services and pay a fraction of the cost? Would this book be worth it if you could focus on just being here in Tulum and enjoying yourself versus trying to hunt down impossible-to-find information?

There are a few goals of this book. This book aims to help you enjoy Tulum with fewer issues while saving money. The goal is to make everything easy to find, understand, and easily accessible. The goal is to share all of the helpful hacks I've learned along the way to give you the best experience in Tulum.

Also, this book aims to help support locals. They don't always have the skills to market their business successfully, so this is just one small way of giving back to support the local community. Thank you for being willing to support local businesses.

I've gotten many recommendations during my time here and it was a challenge trying to decode all the details. This guide will help to simplify the process and give you access to the best recommendations to get acclimated to Tulum.

This book is for anyone who doesn't want to pay an

arm and a leg while visiting or living in Tulum and who wants to simplify the process by skipping the learning curve when coming here.

Anything underlined is clickable so you can access more information about recommendations and access to the locations of places. These local tips will keep you very happy and supported while here. Welcome to Tulum, the place I love getting to call home.

A Note About This Guide

I am simply sharing my experience and what I have learned to be true here in Tulum while I have lived here. We are not liable for anything that happens from the use of this book. By choosing to use these tips, tricks, and tools, you choose to do so at your own risk. If you have a poor experience or notice something that is not accurate, please email alyssac@live.com. Things can change quickly in Tulum, so these updates are helpful. I would be very grateful, as our goal is to ensure this guide is accurate and helpful.

To ensure the accuracy of this guide and provide quick and fast updates if things change, we have created two worksheets available to you that are very important. The first is a Google doc with regular updates just from me and awesome bonuses. You can Scan the QR Code¹ below to access this document.

The second document is available for YOU, the reader, to add any important things you think other readers should know about Tulum that is missing in the book, changes you noticed, or things you've experienced that are life-changing (in a positive way). Please keep it respectful, kind, and light. Scan QR CODE² to access the document!

QR- 1 

QR- 2 

Chapter 1
TULUM BASICS

Patience

This is an important topic to discuss. When in Tulum, it's important to know that this place is growing rapidly, almost too rapidly. Some things here WILL seem backward to you, and some things will feel like they take forever.

Even though it's not an island, it can often feel like it's

island time here. I can also promise you that things will go wrong for you. Things will take longer than you are used to and the challenges here are real. So, when they happen, just remember that it's not that you're the unluckiest human on the planet.

The truth is that it's still just a developing town. Keeping your patience in check will keep things laughable and less chaotic in your mind. Everything is solvable, just in a different and probably slower and more backward way. You will leave Tulum with a stronger patience muscle.

The short answer is yes; you need a visa, and the good news is that you can get one when you enter the country.

There's no application or any pre-work. Mexico gives up to 180 days. It's best to have proof of a lease (you can easily make a pretend one) or a return flight in case they try to hassle you. I've been lucky to not have any issues getting it at the exact time I needed it. It can be hit or miss, though, so it's best to err on the side of caution.

Neighborhoods

These are the main areas of Tulum that you will encounter while living here! These locations are all magical in their own way. Explore the difference in locations while you are here!

El Centro

You will find El Centro area is the closest representative of Mexican culture. There are lots of affordable local shops, activities, and restaurants. You can find street taco vendors here for 50 cents, and you will find a lot of the local population here.

The cost of living is cheaper here, and it is important to always be cautious here from a safety perspective.

Though I wouldn't call it dangerous, and I also wouldn't recommend walking alone at night in certain areas off the main strip.

It will take about 15–20 minutes to the beach without traffic from town.

This location is fairly safe. However, there have been some reports of shootings here. Not a lot, and it can be a little worse during elections. However, Tulum, as a whole, feels safe.

This is the most

expensive part of town and where you will find all the tourists. This part of town has beautiful places to visit and high-end experiences. You will spend a lot of money in this part of town. There are not many places to live and set up for long-term living as it's mostly hotels.

This is a very safe part of town. A few shootings have been reported in Tulum, including a few restaurants down by the beach, but they all revolved around cartel activity and mostly between cartel members. Tourists are not the target (remember that tourists are the client). It hasn't been more than a handful in my year and half of being here. I would not let this deter you from heading to the beach.

La Veleta

This location is very residential. This is tucked away into the jungle and takes about 15–30 minutes to get to the beach from here, depending on how deep into this area you are. You will find lots of nomads and locals in this area. It's right next to El Centro and Aldea Zama. It's a very affordable place to live when it's not high season. Safety-wise, the streets can be very dark at night, and I do not advise walking in the dark. There has been crime reported against tourists in this area.

Roads can be a challenge, with many not paved. Lots of potholes and dusty/dirt roads. I wouldn't live there due to all of the potholes.

This neighborhood is between the beach and El Centro. This is home to many ex-pats. This area is more expensive than in town and La Veleta. It's less expensive than the beach.

This area is fairly safe, but you should always be cautious as many low-wage-earning construction members work here. The streets can be fairly empty. This area is starting to build shops and restaurants, but this is mostly home to housing. The design of homes here is luxurious and beautiful. This is the nicest area in the main area of Tulum (outside of the beach).

Tipping in Tulum

The normal tipping amount in Tulum is between 10%–15%. Because workers here do not get taken care of, I always tip 20%. Take care of the locals; they work hard.

Reliable Wi-Fi?

The short answer is YES! Digital Nomads know Tulum to be a great resource for Wi-Fi. Some people have complained that they could not access strong wi-Fi (I've seen this in ex-pat Facebook groups etc.), and I believe that those people didn't do enough research to know where to go.

I've lived here for a few years and have had zero problems conducting business from here due to the lack of Wi-Fi.

There are certain places you can access Wi-Fi that allows FaceTime and Zoom with ease, and you can access the most popular ones in the next section. You can access other locations outside these co-working spaces where the Wi-Fi is FREE. You can always ask your landlord to upgrade your Wi-Fi if it isn't as fast at home. Also, be sure to ask for Fiberoptic to make sure you have good service.

TIP: Always ask about the MBPS speed before signing a lease. You want to see at least 50 MBPS. The home run is 250 MBPS.

Below is a list of co-working spaces that are my favorite to visit! What's a Co-working space? It's office where other work-from-home folks go to have a place away from home to work.

- Digital Jungle: This place is located in town and is such a beautiful vibe. You can access day passes for as little as $15 a day, weekly passes for as little as $75 a week, or monthly passes for as little as $252 a month! To access more information about Digital Jungle, Scan QR Code below to access![1]

- Co-Working Tulum: The perk here is that you get to work from the most beautiful places in Tulum, AND it's much more affordable than some of the other co-working spaces. You'll pay anywhere from $47–$197 for a week for up to three months! Get more info Scan Qr code below to access[2]! This gives you access to a tribe of humans who pick different locations to co-work together at over 20 of the best Wi-Fi locations in Tulum! They also have other great ways to co-connect through dining, exploring, working out, and more! You can buy day, weekly, and monthly passes, including unlimited scanning and a certain number of copies and prints. The monthly membership also gives you up to 7 hours of meeting room use, perfect for start-up businesses.

QR- 1 

QR- 2 

Additionally, you can rent private offices for any duration between 4 hours to one month.

- Los Amigos: This place is located in the La Veleta neighborhood and is another co-working place.To get more details Scan Qr code below[1] by connecting through WhatsApp! Be sure to check out their EPIC spa and rock-climbing wall.

  - Daily: $10 USD

  - Weekly: $40 USD (meeting room, 60 min)

  - Monthly: $150 USD(meeting room, 60 min)

Each plan includes coffee and water and access to a printer. It's open from 9:00 a.m. to 6:00 p.m. every day. However, if you pay for a membership, you have access to the space 24 hours a day. They have fiber optic Wi-Fi at 40 megabits per second.

- Selina: Want to co-work down at the beach? This is your spot. Here's a fun hack! If you ever feel like

QR- 1 

you need to know if you are going to a place in the world with good Wi-Fi, check to see if there is a Selina in the area. They are global and insanely reliable with Wi-Fi! The cost at the beach is always a little higher, but it's worth being able to walk out to the ocean. Scan Qr code below to access.[1]

- $15 a day

- 72 USD/week

- 236/month

- Huaya Camp: This is a little private oasis! For only 10 dollars a day, you can work in a private co-working space in nature, right in el Centro. This is a little magical spot under the radar! Go see the magic of this spot. It's a hidden secret that no one knows about! Scan Qr code below to access[2] to access.

QR- 1 

QR- 2

- Ki'bok:

- Day Pass: $12 USD (Terrace Access)

- Weekly Pass: $75 USD (Terrace & Conference Room Access)

- Conference Room: $10 USD per hour

- Skype Booth: $10 USD per hour

- Monthly Membership: $200 USD

The pros of working at Ki'bok are that they have fast Wi-Fi at 150 megabits per second, and it's right in the center of Tulum. Scan Qr code below to access. [1]

Want more options? This app has lots of workspace options. Scan Qr code below[2] to access it!

Reliable Wi-Fi for Free At These Locations

There are places where you can get reliable Wi-Fi and NOT pay a fee. That's right, enjoy these places for free! Here is a list of magical cafes and restaurants with excellent Wi-Fi without paying anything to visit! For some of these, you may need to purchase something from the restaurant. Click the name to access it!

- Hotel Muare (La Veleta)[3]

QR– 1

QR– 2

QR– 3

- **Norita (Aldea Zama):** If you go there, the day beds on the side of the pool are for hotel guests and you don't need to purchase food when sitting there.

- **Mia (Beach):** If you sit on the couches to the side of the restaurant, and enter from the side instead of the front, you shouldn't have to pay for anything, and can work there with no issues. They also have a cool pizza bar area, a library/movie theater, and some hidden coves all around the resort so be sure to have a look around to find the comfiest spot to work from.

- **Layla (El Centro):** This place is so affordable and delicious. Food is really cheap and yummy. It's expected that you purchase something, however, they are pretty laid back.

- **Orchard House (Aldea Zama)**

Norita (Aldea Zama):	
Mia (Beach):	
Layla (El Centro):	
Orchard House (Aldea Zama)	

- Kanan (Beach): There are lots of little nooks and areas you can easily work from here without having to buy something. This place is so beautiful, a true work of art.

- Encanto Cantina (El Centro)

- Girafe Restuarant (Tuk Tulum– Centro)

- Ikal: You can easily work from here without being hassled to purchase anything. I love working from the treehouse or the yoga shala when class isn't happening on a comfy pillow pile.

Kanan (Beach):	
Encanto Cantina (El Centro)	
Girafe Restuarant (Tuk Tulum– Centro)	
Ikal:	

WIFI Passwords List In Tulum

Here is a list of 45+ Wi–Fi passwords in Tulum to access Wi–Fi anywhere you go. Scan Qr code below to access[1]!

QR– 1 

Mailing in Tulum

Getting things mailed in Tulum can be a nightmare. Get ready for an import tax if you want something mailed to you from the states. I once paid 150 USD in customs fees when the package was only worth $40 USD. You can also have things get stuck in customs. I know a few friends who have been waiting five months to get their items out of customs. So, I avoid having anything sent directly here because of these disasters.

To avoid the annoyance and nightmare, use the following hacks:

Ask those in local Facebook groups to mule whatever you need from the states. Girl Gang Facebook Group is a great place to ask, and Facebook has about ten others as well! Click HERE to access it! Our community is supportive. Maybe you make a trade or just ask for a favor.

There is a company that you can ship your belongings to in Texas, and then they will bring items over the border for you! You can order from any store or send personal belongings. This is the best way to avoid customs. The only things you can't send are drugs, items containing CBD or THC, guns, gun accessories, knives, animals, dangerous items, chemicals, and a few other specific items. The number to contact these people is +52–461–105–5523. The delivery price is 800 pesos for SMALL packages from 1 to 5 kg. After 5 kg, the cost is $115 per kg (the size can determine the cost as well)

Mail Sent To Tulum

- Option 1: Savana

Maybe you want to take the risk and have something delivered here. If so, there are some important things to know.

The first is that you want to have a solid place to have it delivered to. Your safest bet is ordering it to Savana to make sure there is someone to sign and receive your package, so it's not lost upon delivery.

To receive packages in Savana it costs 50 pesos or 100 pesos depending on the size. It is important that you put Savanna's address, your name, and telephone number.

Shipping address

Alyssa Cavosie (ally) Selina Tulum
Carr. Tulum-Boca Paila Km. 7.5, Tulum Beach, Zona
Hotelera
TULUM CENTRO
TULUM, QUINTANA ROO 77760
Mexico

- Option 2: Selina

You can also have it mailed to Selina, where their security will receive the package. There is no fee to have it received, and you can just say you are a guest of the hotel.

The one place I will order from without worry in Tulum is Amazon. You can use Amazon since they have their delivery and service in Mexico. You will most likely pay extra import fees, but you will know the cost upfront, which is great.

Please see the photo below of how I placed Selina's address into the Amazon address bar if you want to send anything there. If you order from amazon, this is how it should look when sending (you can use this as a map for other addresses to have an idea of how it looks since it most likely will look different than your home country.

Mail Sent From Tulum

Goto DHL in the center of town to ship out! Scan Qr code below to access.[1]

Shopping In Tulum

Shopping in Tulum is limited. You can buy really

QR- 1 

expensive clothing on the beach road. You can buy much less expensive stuff on the main road in El Centro. However, you will not find any mainstream stores.

You will need to go to Playa Del Carmen, which is one hour away and a $2.50 Collectivo van ride away. They have stores like Walmart, Forever 21, Pet Smart, Sam's Club, Old Navy, Nike, Adidas, Zara, etc. There are so many options; these are just a few examples. It's nice sometimes to have the comforts of home so close to you. See how to ride the Collectivo in the vehicles section!

You will quickly learn that Tulum has no news stations to easily find out what's going on. Also, with Tulum being relatively small, it's easy for rumors to run wild. That's why these resources are REALLY helpful. These two links will support you in getting accurate and up-to-date information here in Tulum. Scan Qr code below to access[1] Tulum Al Minuto and Scan Qr code below to access[2] the NotITulum Facebook page.

Do I Need To Speak Spanish In Tulum?

It is not vital to speak Spanish in Tulum because so many people here speak English. However, it is helpful to have some Spanish under your belt. You will encounter locals who do not speak English in local stores and restaurants.

Google Translate will be your best friend in these situations. Know the special features it offers to make your life way easier. There is a photo button that will take a photo of a menu or label and change the words into English. It's seriously magic. If you need to have a conversation, you can click the "conversation" button, select "Spanish," and have the person speak in Spanish

QR- 1 

QR- 2 

into the phone. The app will translate it so you can read whatever they spoke into the phone in English.

For some of the services in this book, you will need to use this tool. I promise that while it can be a little challenging, it's possible, especially with this tool. Don't shy away from supporting the locals due to language barriers. Technology will support you in overcoming this hurdle! You've got this!

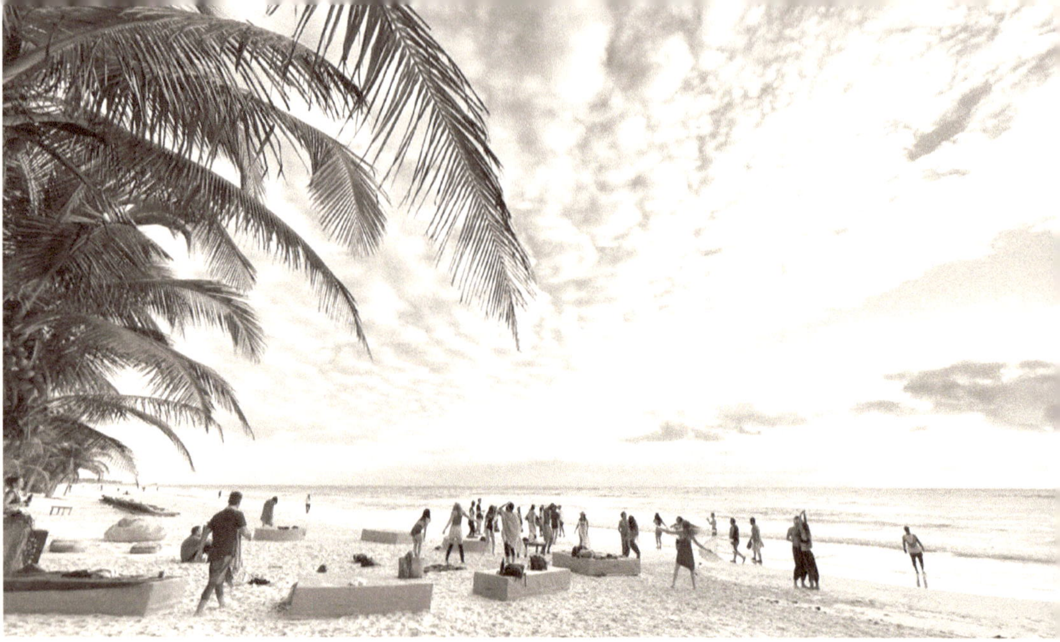

Chapter 2
MONEY

Managing ATMs in Tulum can be tricky! Order a Charles Swab card to get free ATM withdrawal if you're from the USA. For more info on this, reference the Inside Out Travel Guide accessed by Scanning Qr code below.[1]

QR- 1 

Cheapest ATM to pull money: Super Aki grocery store

This ATM is only 30 pesos to pull money from. The max is 4k pesos.

Most Expensive: The bank next to Super AKI. This ATM charges 150 pesos, and you can only pull 3,000 pesos, and you can only pull money twice. I would avoid this place at all costs.

Where can I pull the most money? The HSBC ATM in Chedruai is incredible! It's 80 pesos a pull. However, you can pull 7,000 pesos at a time. There are also two other ATMs there, so you can have way more pulls from the ATM if you need to get additional cash.

Want tips on safety with ATMs when traveling the

world? Please check out The Inside Out Travelers Guide by Scanning Qr code below.[1]

Paying For Stuff

Understanding how to pay for things here in Tulum will be very helpful for you.

Credit Cards: You can use a credit card almost anywhere. I usually carry a VISA as it's most widely accepted. I use Chase Sapphire because there are no foreign transactions fees. Many credit cards won't have foreign transaction fees associated, so be sure to get one before visiting. Street vendors will only accept cash, and some smaller stores will charge 3% to 5% for using a credit card. Anytime you are asked to pay in pesos or USD, always pick pesos because you will often get charged a high rate for the exchange.

QR– 1 

Cash: I always carry a small amount of cash with me because you will need this for taxis, paying entry fees for certain events, sharing bills at dinner, and other little situations you wouldn't expect.

ATMs: I always use ATMs to take cash out. I use a debit card from Charles Schwab that refunds any ATM fees, which is epic. Make sure

to sort out getting this card before you come. There are also many other options like this, and I highly suggest carrying a card like this. Never have them convert your currency; they charge high prices. Always keep it in pesos; never have the bank convert for your ATM machine. If you see anything about converting on the ATM, always answer no.

Money Exchange: Avoid these places! These have high transaction fees. Stick to ATMs. Also, there are minimal ATMs on the beach road, so make sure to get your cash in town first.

Calculating USD To Pesos

Here are two easy hacks on easily calculating USD to Pesos without needing a currency converter.

Option 1

- Memorize the following:

- 20 pesos = $1

- 100 pesos = $5

- 500 pesos =$25

- 1000 pesos = $50

- 2000 pesos = $100

OR

Option 2

You can divide the number of pesos by two and take off the zero to get the USD calculation.

Example 1: 500 pesos divided by 2 = 250. Then, take off the zero, and it's $25 USD.

Example 2: 2000 pesos divided by 2 = 1000··· Then, take off one zero, and it's $100 USD.

Have you ever come across a situation where you meet a traveler from a different country and want to give them money electronically but are not sure how?

I've got a few tips that will make your life much easier. There are a few apps that will make this incredibly easy. Just download either Wise or Revolt. Revolt is free to transfer money, and Wise is only a few dollars. This will be way cheaper than using places like Western Union and more convenient. Anyone with a bank account and a mobile phone can use this. This is great if you split dinner, need to pay rent, or pay for anything else.

Need to sign up for Revolt? Scan Qr code below.[1]

Need to sign up for Transferwise? Scan Qr code below.[2]

QR- 1 

QR- 2 

Chapter 3
ACTIVITIES & COMMUNITIES

Here is a list of awesome things you can do while in Tulum. There is no shortage of fun things to do in this town.

I've watched Tulum violently kick people out because

those people did not respect the lands. These people would have all sorts of challenges and curveballs thrown at them. The best way to experience a smooth transition into Tulum is to go to the ruins and ask permission to be here. Do a meditation, give thanks, feel gratitude in your heart, and watch a smooth experience in Tulum unfold.

A Must-Have App

I recently came across a must-have app. This is the most accurate and comprehensive guide regarding cenotes, upcoming events, beach clubs, and workspaces. They are building and adding more to this app every single day. Scan Qr code below[1] to download this app.

Salsa and Bachata Guide

Want to experience the culture of Mexico? Make sure to get your dancing in! You can explore Salsa in a classroom setting or explore it in a social setting. Please

QR- 1 

Scan Qr code below[1] to find out about everything Salsa related.

Okay, so here are my go-to spots for classes! You'll find yoga, sound healing, fitness, dance, and more!

Holistika: This has the most amazing and beautiful setting. This place will charge more for classes, but you can get a good deal with a local ID. The cost for a local ID is 1800 pesos ($90 USD). See the getting

QR- 1 

a local ID section of the book. You can check their website for their schedule by Scanning Qr code below[1]. Also, want to speak to a human to ask questions? Here is their number! Scan Qr code below[2] to message them on Whatsapp!

Om Collective: Can you say, "donation-based classes"? They have classes Monday–Sunday at 8 am, 10 am, 6 pm, and 8 pm! Want to get their class schedule? Message them on IG at @OM.Collective.Tulum. Scan Qr code below[3] for their location.

Ikal: This is my beach spot! They have an awesome vibe and the best outdoor studio overlooking the beach. They have discounts for locals for about 150 pesos a class and 250 pesos for non–locals. Want the schedule?

QR- 1 

QR- 2

QR- 3

Head to their website by Scanning Qr code below[1]! Scan Qr code below[2] for their location.

Here are a few of the ones I've visited and enjoyed. These are more local cenotes and are, of course, affordable!

- Cenote Cristal & Cenote Escondido: Scan Qr code below[3] to access Escondido, and across the street is Cenote Cristal. These are very low-key and have a local feel. These won't be overrun by tourists, and you can visit both in a day since they are across the street from each other. These are worth a visit! The cost is under $10 USD for both.

QR- 1

QR- 2

QR- 3

- Vesica: This place is beautiful! Scan Qr code below[1] to locate. This cenote has a restaurant, day beds, and Wi-Fi! You can go work for the day or relax. This has a 150 pesos entrance fee and should not be missed. Note that some beds have minimum spend & some don't.

- Cenote Car Wash: This cenote is beautiful and worth a visit. This has a local feel. Be sure to bring your snorkel gear! Scan Qr code below to access.[2]

There is a secret cenote in the ocean at Selina. Bring snorkel gear and see if you can find it. This is one of the smallest and most unknown cenotes in Tulum! It's in between the yoga shala and the restaurant.

Want more cenote options? Access our resource guide

QR- 1 

QR- 2

by Scanning Qr code below.[1] Or, check out our favorite Tulum app by by Scanning Qr code below[2]. This app has the best guide for cenotes.

Here is a list of the best places in Tulum to take the best Instagram photos. Click the name to access the location. Some of these are free and some will have an entrance fee.

- Swings at Coco Tulum Beach Club
- Selina Tulum
- Vagalume Beach Club
- Conestesia Bunny at the Entrance of Conestesia
- Follow That Dream Sign
- Azulik Tulum
- Kin Toh

QR– 1 

QR– 2 

- Crooked Palm Tree on Playa Paraiso

- Casa Malca – Pablo Escobar Mansion

- ROC Luxe Tulum

- Matcha Mama

- Cenote Calavera

- Cenote Dos Ojos

- Gran Cenote

- Papaya Playa Project

- Nomade

- Raw Love

- Tulum Ruins

- Playa Santa Fe on Abandoned Boats

Tourist Activities

So, the following activities are either free, affordable, or must-do activities. Now, I'm not huge on Touristy activities, but I've done a handful in my time here and know most people like them. So, here are my top picks.

Best Photo Spot QRS

Swings At Coco Tulum

Vagalume Beach Club

Selina

Contestesia Bunny

update: This location is now closed

Follow that Dream

Azulik

Kin Tok

Crooked Palm Tree

Casa Malca

ROC Luxe Tulum

Matcha Mama beach

Matcha Mama Town

Best Photo Spot QRS

Holistika Art Walk:

This is like a little piece of Burning Man in Tulum. This is so cool, and it's free. When you get to Holistika, you will need to go to the back. Insider Tip: Look for the sign that says "Art Walk." I first thought their common ground was the art walk because it was so beautiful. Scan Qr code below[1] to locate it!

Bike Ride To Sian Ka'an: There are

QR- 1

many ways to go to Sian Kan, but take a bicycle if you want a bit of an adventure! Rent a bicycle and ride 55 minutes down the hotel zone road. Sian Kan is stunning and not worth missing. Be sure to go earlier in the morning or later to avoid the intense heat mid-day. Scan Qr code below[1] to access Sian Ka'an and Scan Qr code[2] to see where the beach road is!

Visiting The Ruins: Now, this is a staple for most tourists. This will cost you about $5 USD. Make sure to ask the lands for permission to be in Tulum when you arrive at the ruins! Scan Qr code below[3] to access it!

Mystika: Experience: Mystika is a one-of-a-kind sensory experience designed to take the viewer on a journey of connection with Mayan cosmology, the

QR- 1

QR- 2

QR- 3

most impressive natural sanctuaries in Mexico, and the spiritual power of horses: totems of healing, wisdom, and evolution. In other words, go check out this psychedelic art museum. The cost is $20 USD. Scan Qr code below[1] to access it!

Xel-Ha Eco-adventure Park: This place is a little more pricey. However, this place is an all-day activity. For $100 USD, you can snorkel, check out a lighthouse that's 30 meters high and then take the slide down, then ride down the lazy river on a tube. Check out a Mayan cave and cliff jump. Try not to fall when crossing two parallel ropes suspended above the water. Enjoy a zip line that will end with a fun landing in the refreshing waters of the Xel-Há River. Swing from a rope and then drop into the refreshing waters of a cavern, check out the jungle

QR- 1

trails, walk on the floating bridge, take a bike ride to explore nature, or fly a kite! Click Scan Qr code below[1] to access it!

Explore the town: This is free. You can walk the main road to check out the little shops and restaurants! Scan Qr code below[2] to access a starting point on the main road!

Temezcal Experiences

So, you may be wondering what a Temezcal is. This is a must-try spiritual and cultural activity in Tulum. This is a ceremony steeped in Mexican heritage. It involves participants sitting in a traditional sweat lodge for health and therapeutic benefits. Ceremonies usually last for two or more hours and are typically led by a sort of spiritual leader called a shaman or temazcalero.

It has been practiced by Mexicans in that part of the

QR- 1 

QR- 2 

world and other parts of the world for thousands of years.

The prices for Temezcal range SO much. Some can be $80 USD or more, especially at the beach. So, I will give you access to two locations with the most authentic, local feel and the best prices.

The first place is Botanica! The cost is 250 pesos for locals and 500 pesos for nonlocals. I don't believe you need to show your local ID here. They have Temezcal Monday and Wednesday at 7 pm. They also have a Sunday at 10 am. Message them on IG for more info: @BotanicaTulum. The location can be accessed by Scanning Qr code below[1].

The second location, and also my favorite location, is Espiritu Wellness. For visitors is $30 USD, and for locals, it's 250 pesos with a local ID. The reason it's my favorite is because they have great English translators,

QR– 1 

and there are always fewer people here. The location can be accessed by Scanning Qr code below[1].

Plant Medicine Experiences

This topic is a really important one to discuss. Plant medicine is widely available in Tulum. Many claim to be healers, and it's important to make sure you are going with real shamans who will keep you safe during the experience and who you can trust. There have been healers who have done more harm than good and who have used shamanism as a reason to cross sexual boundaries or simply to profit. It is a very big deal to embark on a plant medicine journey, and you want to take it seriously.

Here are some important things to note and some red flags to look out for when choosing a healer or shaman.

- It's a red flag if the facilitator uses fear or flattery to attract you. That could mean telling you that they can see much negative energy around you

QR– 1 

or in your life and, if you don't let them heal you, you will never find peace or love. Another tactic is praying on vulnerability with flattery. For example, "you have a beautiful light, you're full of potential, but you need this medicine to bring it out, or you won't be able to share your gifts with the world. You need me to help you with that."

- It's a red flag if they are vague about how they learned to deliver the medicine or are "self-taught." Guides should be able to tell you who they apprenticed with to learn the medicine, how long they have been practicing and why they are qualified to offer the ceremony.

- Predatory behavior includes: offering you private "love magic" or "sexual chakra" healing, advising you that their wife doesn't mind them being with other people, being overly friendly and too touchy or "handsy" with you. They might try to separate you from the group or offer you 1:1 sexual healing.

- It's a red flag if you notice grandiose and egocentric behavior. They claim that there is nothing the medicine can't fix. If you take it with them, it fixes all your problems.

- If they let you take medicine, no questions asked, it's a red flag. For example, a good facilitator will ask: When was your last ceremony? Are you taking any SSRIs? Do you have bipolar or schizophrenia? They will ask these to protect your wellbeing.

- Pay attention to spiritual bypassing, like if they have trouble being in reality or accountable for their actions. They believe they are a spiritual being above human attachments.

- You can ask in Tulum about the person's reputation within Tulum Facebook groups and by asking locals. Do this to make sure they have a good reputation. Don't seek out a shaman on Instagram or Google. Ask locals for

support on finding those recommended by multiple people.

- It's really important to trust your gut; it's ok to back away if something feels off.

- Be wary of shamans who don't enforce the pre-diet leading up to the ceremony.

Always Ask The Following:

- How does this person's energy feel & do you feel safe in their energy?

- Do I feel supported?

- Where is the location?

- Who will be holding space during and after your ceremony?

- Is there a feminine/masculine energy balance?

- For male shamans (it is always a red flag if they offer medicine alone and without the presence of at least one woman).

- Ask them how they started on their path with medicine and why.

If you want more information on finding safe shamans and healers as a woman, there is a WhatsApp group you can access by Scanning Qr code below[1].

I hope this helps, and remember to be smart, cautious, aware, and safe.

QR– 1 

Tulum Beach Insider Tips

So, navigating the beach in Tulum can be a little tricky. Many places will deny you access to the beach unless you are willing to pay. This isn't technically allowed, but Tulum is sometimes like the wild west. There are some tips and tricks to this that will support you in having a seamless and smooth experience on the beach.

The first thing to understand is that there are two sides to the beach: the north and south sides. The north side has more public access, more locals, and lower prices. It's to the left if you look at the ocean from town on a map. Always be careful with parking down here, so you don't get towed.

You may think that you have to pay to go to the beach; however, this isn't true. You need to know these hacks. I've never paid to go to the beach in two years of living here.

Scooter Or Car To The Beach?

It's recommended to take a scooter because traffic can cost you hours of waiting to get there, especially in high

season. With a scooter, you can easily and quickly drive past the traffic.

Option 1: Bring a beach blanket and a cooler, and set up in the sand. This is a free way of enjoying the beach!

Option 2: Rent a daybed or cabana (this will have a minimum spend on food and drinks). Selina is my favorite if you want to stay within budget. The bed costs can vary depending on where you go. It could be $50 USD or $250 USD. The

prices will change based on day and season. The best way to find a spot is to drive to Selina, park in the parking lot for free, walk down the strip, see which vibe you like best, and just ask about the cost of a bed.

Option 3: Book your stay in a hotel with a beach club. This will be the priciest and will be the most convenient.

Easy Entrance At The Beach Clubs

Want to access the beach and avoid being hassled? Maybe there's a certain area of the beach you want to access. Well, here are some insider tips on how to do so. Click the name of the location below to get linked directly to it!

Selina: I love Selina! It's a little slice of heaven and so beautiful! I love it here. The parking here is free and then when you get there, instead of walking through the restaurant, walk on the path to

Selina	
Papaya Playa Project	
Delek	
Ahau	
Posada Margarita	
Pocna	
Ikal	

the left of reception and the restaurant. You will be able to access the beach with no hassle directly. There are also day beds that line the pool. These are for Selina guests. However, no one ever checks, so head to Selina if you want a free day bed! Make sure to get there a bit earlier, though, because they will fill up.

Papaya Playa Project: This place you can access by saying you are headed to the restaurant. Then, you can easily just head down to the beach. There are places along the beach to set up a beach blanket to enjoy the day.

Delek: This is another easy entry point to enjoy the beach. They will not try to charge you a minimum

spend to access the beach. Also, you can get a free day bed here if they are not reserved.

Ahau: Ahau is the same as Delek. These places are more laid back. You can say you are headed to the restaurant and then head to the beach.

Posada Margarita: So, I haven't personally tried this one yet; however, my friend shared that this is an easy access point, and you can enter without a hassle.

Pocna: Another easy place to access the beach from!

Ikal: Ikal is my go-to spot.75% of the year, you can park for free with a scooter. You can also park for free if you attend a class or make a purchase from the restaurant when they are charging. I feel safe parking here. On the beach road, it's really easy to get towed, so I stick to parking with restaurants. I know I am protected at Ikal, and I like that!

Free Public Beaches

If you want to avoid the hassle of getting access to the beach, you can easily visit these four public access beaches. Just note that some of these you will pay for parking. For example, Playa Santa Fe is a $10 USD fee.

- Playa Santa Fe | Santa Fe Beach
- Playa Pescadores | Fisherman's Beach
- Playa Paraiso | Paradise Beach
- Playa las Palmas

Here is a link that will instantly help you connect to our unique communities in Tulum! Scan Qr code below[1] to access our document that has 34+ Whatsapp Chat groups for all of the different community groups and activities in Tulum! This will make sure you quickly and easily connect to the magical community here in Tulum. This will give you access to people, activities, and events.

Tulum attracts some of the most unique and special

QR- 1 

humans here, and there are tons of epic events, communities, and people to experience.

Women In Tulum

Do you want to feel super connected with a high vibe tribe of women here in Tulum? Want to feel safe knowing other women who are here in the community? Be sure to join the Tulum Girl Gang! Welcome to the Girl Gang. To get linked into our community, the first step is heading over to our website to join by Scanning Qr code below[1].

They have in-person AND online meetups! Scan Qr code below[2] for the Facebook group. Scan Qr cod[3] for their IG.

QR- 1 

QR- 2

QR- 3

Chapter 4

BEST AND CHEAPEST LIST

In Tulum, the prices range from low to high. Tourist traps are everywhere, so this guide will save you so much money because you will know exactly what to avoid. Here are the best local places with local prices that I love! Just because they are cheap doesn't mean they can't be the best! All these are things I've tried and currently use. I do not get paid to recommend these locations. Know where to go and who to trust!

Best Vegan/Veg Food:

These are the places you can usually find me. Light, bright, and delicious!

- Holistika: They serve breakfast, lunch, and dinner. They do a killer vegan cookie. Go for breakfast to get the French toast and the tofu scramble. Incredible. Chia seed bowl is also amazing. Be sure to check out the art walk as well here. This place is an experience you must not miss. Food and drink options range from 90 pesos to 300 pesos. Scan Qr code below[1] to access.

- The Real Coconut: This place is down on the beach. It's absolutely stunning. Food can be hit or miss because it's healthy. Be sure to check it out. Avocado toast is delicious. A yoga class here with some breakfast is a great way to do it. Food and

QR- 1

drink options range from 100 pesos to 500 pesos. Scan Qr code below[1] to access. They also have an in town location too.

- Matcha Mama: The best smoothie bowls are here. Do not skip a visit for a cool setting and amazing smoothie bowl. They have a location in town, at the beach, and Aldea Zama! Food and drink options range from 50 pesos to 300 pesos. Scan Qr code below[2] to access.

- Raw Love: Another favorite. I love their food more than their smoothies and smoothie bowls. The raw pizza, curry, pad Thai, and energy balls are incredible. They have a location

QR- 1

QR- 2

at the beach in Ahau and town! Food and drink options range from 90 pesos to 300 pesos. Scan Qr code below[1] to access.

Best Pizza

There are a few spots in Tulum that have EPIC pizza. Being a New Yorker, I have a high standard for pizza. A personal pizza will cost you around $10 USD here. Click the names below to access these spots!

QR– 1 

Pizza Papi:[1] This is VEGAN pizza and a must-try. It's unique and delicious.

La Hydra: Scan Qr code below[2] to access.

Pizzeria 85x ciento: Scan Qr code[3] below to access.

Manglar: Scan Qr code[4] below to access.

I lived in India for four months and found the best Indian food I've ever tried in Tulum, Mexico. Go figure. The place is called India Express Curry House. This is a little pricier for delivery, but I highly recommend it. They only do delivery here, and it is a must-try while

QR- 1 

QR- 2

QR- 3

QR- 4

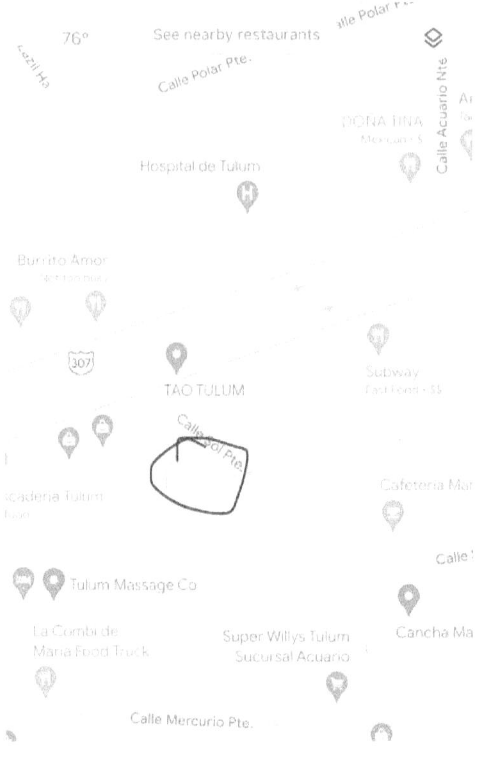

here in Tulum. You can find them by Scanning Qr code below[1]. You can order on Tomato. mx.

The Cheapest Tacos

Maybe you want a late-night snack or just want really cheap food. Whichever it is, head to Scan Qr code[2] for a street that has lots of tacos, and other food. This is some of the cheapest in town. Make sure to try the jackfruit vegan tacos if the vegan cart is there!

QR- 1 

QR- 2

I LOVE fresh juice and coconut water. This place is a hidden gem where you can get a big bottle of coconut water for 50 pesos and a big bottle of juice for 40 pesos. They have orange, green, watermelon, papaya, beet, carrot, and lulu fruit juice. All are yummy! The location isn't accessible on Google maps, but the photo on the map here will guide you to the spot. I also did a location tag HERE[1] at Burrito Amor, across the street.

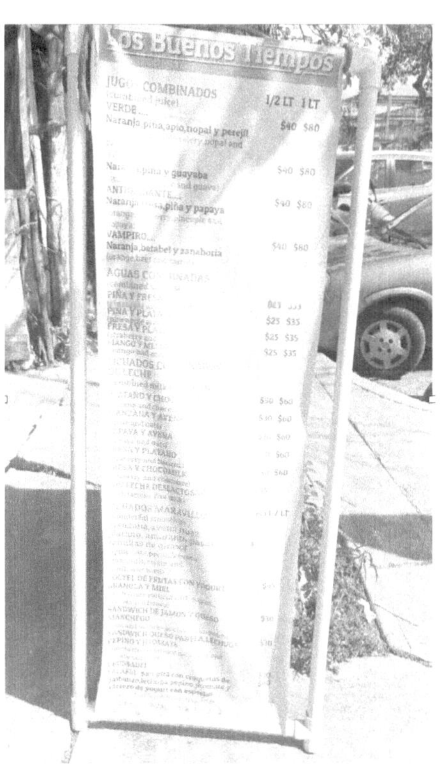

Im adding one more option here if you like your juices made in front of you and if you want

QR– 1

more options. These guys are great and so affordable! Please note they close at 1pm certain days. Click Scan QR Code below[1] to access it.

Restaurants In Town: Affordable, Best Vibe, & Best Food

This is a list of restaurants I love going to because they have the best food, the best ambiance, and affordable prices. Some of these aren't the cheapest, but they are still very affordable for budget-friendly folks. You can easily pay $20 USD to $60 USD at the beach for a meal. So, these prices are manageable compared to some of the other places in Tulum. Make sure to have cash on you; some of these don't accept credit cards or will charge you a fee for using a card. Click the name to access it!

Pasha[2]: This is a Mediterranean Middle Eastern restaurant. They have the best mezzo platters, and

QR- 1

QR- 2

this place is such a vibe. It's a bit pricier than the other restaurants on this list, but I'd be doing you a disservice by leaving it out since it's wonderful.

Palma Central:[1] This place has about 15 food trucks to choose from and live music almost every night of the week. You can catch me here on Tuesdays for Salsa night! Everything is super affordable, costing

QR- 1 

you between $1 USD & $12 USD per meal, depending on what you buy. You could pay one dollar for a taco, $10 for a salad, or $10 for pad Thai. You could pay $4 for French fries. There is something for everyone. This place is such a vibe.

Restuarant Tierra: This place is so beautiful. Located inside Holistika, this place has healthy and delicious food with the best ambiance. It's mostly a vegan menu with some non-veg options too! Scan QR Code below[1] to access it.

Botanica: This is such a beautiful space to eat. It's such a vibe and very affordable. Be sure to check it out! Scan QR Code below[2] to access it.

Burrito Amor: This is a favorite of locals and tourists alike. A trip is not complete without having a burrito from Burrito Amor. The venue isn't super swanky, but

QR- 1 

QR- 2

you will leave with a happy belly and a happy wallet. Burritos cost around $10 USD. Scan QR Code below[1] to access it.

Tres Galeones: Okay, this place is so pretty and romantic. It's a great spot for a date. This one has an extra special memory for me when a date walked out on me in the middle of an argument and short-changed me for the bill. Regardless, I still love this place. Meals here are about $7-$10 USD. Scan QR Code below[2] to access

Los Aguachiles: This place is a hidden gem. It's a seafood restaurant and very affordable. I'm not a huge seafood person, so the fact that this is on my list is a big deal. It's not a fancy ambiance here. However, you will love the food. Don't order this as takeout; it's not quite the same.

QR- 1 

QR- 2

Restaurant at Gypsea Market: This restaurant is strangely not on Google maps; however, it's healthy and delicious. They have tables with swings as seats which makes it a vibe. Scan QR Code below[1] to access it!

Italdo: This is the cutest and most delicious cafe in Tulum. Great for breakfast for some coffee, a pastry, fresh bread, breakfast sandwich, a pizza at lunch, a cake for dessert, and more. They make everything from scratch, and the prices are between $2 USD for a coffee and up to $10 USD for a pizza.

QR– 1 

Acqua & Farina: This is where you want to get your Italian fix. The food is delicious, and it's such a cute spot—food costs between $5 USD and $10 USD. Scan QR Code below[1] to access it!

La Guarida: This place is a vibe!! It's got games and live music every night. Super affordable food and a must-visit that's definitely under the radar. Most dishes are under $10 USD.

When you go to the beach, you will quickly learn it is way more expensive in town. So, if you're

QR- 1 

Restuarant Tierra	
Botanica	
Burrito Amor	
Tres Galeones	
Los Aguachiles	
Restaurant at Gypsea Market	
Italdo	
Acqua & Farina	
La Guarida	

down that way and don't want to spend an arm and a leg, you can access these five spots for delicious and cheap food. Just note that overall, the less expensive side of the beach is the Northside of the beach where Ikal is. Click below to locate.

Raw Love: This is healthy vegan food and smoothies with the cutest setup. Meals are around 200 pesos or $10 USD. Scan QR Code below[1] to access it.

La Malinche Tulum: This place is roadside; however, these tacos are incredible. You can get a meal for about $10–$15 USD. Scan QR Code below[2] to access it.

Matcha Mama: This place is more about smoothie bowls and smoothies, but they offer affordable options

QR– 1 

QR– 2

for around $10 USD. The place is also very cute! Scan QR Code below[1] to access it.

Ikal: This is a fun place to hang out and is my go-to beach spot for beach days. They have a pretty affordable menu for being a restaurant on the beach. This is the most restaurant-like on the entire list here. Scan QR Code below[2] to access it.

Bula Tulum Kava & Kratom: This location is AMAZING. It has kratom drinks which are healthy drinks that have health and energy boosting benefits. They have a beautiful private cenote, and it's a wonderful vibe to experience. They also have delicious sandwiches and apps. Scan QR Code below[3] to access it.

QR- 1 

QR- 2

QR- 3

Ice Cream: Cheapest & Best

This place has the cheapest cones in town! Pay 25 pesos for a cone which is a little over $1. You can pay up to 100 pesos or $5 USD at some tourist ice cream shops. Scan QR Code below[1] to locate it!

Rapid Covid Test: Cheapest And Easiest Way To Get A Covid Test

So, if you need a 24-hour test (PCR), you will find these locations all around Tulum. However, if you need a rapid test (Antigen), you can do it right at the airport. They have the cheapest and easiest way of doing this. There is never really a line; just get there 30–45 minutes early.

There are available modules at terminals 2,3 and 4 to get tested. These mobile units operate from 6:00 a.m. to 9:00 p.m.

The cost is $17 USD or 290 MXN.

QR- 1 

This is much cheaper than in Tulum. Costs for the test are much more.

This is by far the most reliable way to get your covid test. If you want the safety of doing it in advance, my go to spot is outside Chedraui for about $30 USD.

I drop my laundry off with Yazmin at Lavanderia Sol. The location is Scan QR Code below[1], which is right in town. The cost is 18/KG, so a big laundry bag is about

QR– 1 

$5 dollars. She never ruined or lost anything either, which is HUGE.

She also does alterations and shoe cleaning. For alterations, it cost me a few dollars to take in a dress when I lost weight. She returned my shoe's color back to white. To contact her: Scan QR Code below[1] to message them on WhatsApp.

Mechanic: Most Affordable And Most Trustworthy

So, my go-to guy is Ivan. He has the best prices, and more importantly, I TRUST him. He and his dad are locals in town, and I LOVE supporting them. They are quick too. To contact Ivan, message him on WhatsApp by Scanning QR Code below[2].

I think it's always important to have two mechanics especially in case of an emergency. Here is my other

QR- 1 

QR- 2 

go-to mechanic. It's called 2lumMotors. This spot is great because they are always quick to answer, and the owner speaks English. So, while this isn't the cheapest, it's still affordable and they also guarantee their work which is awesome. Scan QR Code below[1] to message Angel, the owner of this location.

You can get a massage for 800 pesos ($40 USD) for an hour, and they even come to your home! To schedule, Whatsapp her by scanning QR Code below[2].

For about 1000 pesos, you can get a healing massage

QR- 1 

QR- 2 

with local Mayans—message on WhatsApp by Scanning QR Code below[1].

Acupuncture: Cheapest And Best

For $12.50 USD a session (250 pesos), you can get acupuncture here in Tulum! Reach out to Mari to schedule by Scanning QR Code below[2]!

Scooter Rental: Cheapest And Best

Want a cheap Moto to rent? Reach out to Ally. Mention this guide, and you will receive the Moto for $20 a day over a week of usage! To contact Ally, Message on Whatsapp by Scanning QR Code below[3]. Normally, the minimum cost is $25 USD a day.

QR- 1 

QR- 2 

QR- 3 

Want to get copies and not pay 50 cents a page at Digital Jungle? There is a location in town where copies cost 2 pesos (10 cents) and printing a sheet cost 3 pesos (15 cents). The location is below[1]! Save LOTS of money by going to this local spot!

Access 3 hours at this lux spa. It's called Leafs, and for 3 hours, the cost is $27.50 USD (550 Mexican pesos). To reserve, Whatsapp them by Scanning QR Code below[2]. Scan QR Code below[3] to see more about it on the website. You will be in heaven.

QR- 1 

QR- 2

QR- 3

Hardware Store: Cheap Alert

Okay, so there are many cheap hardware stores all over Tulum, but you can Scan QR Code below[1] to access my goto one. I've gotten random things like keychains, tools, duck tape, and even a machete (not for my ex, only for coconuts). These guys have all sorts of little odds and ends.

Kitchen Supplies: Cheapest

Scan QR Code below[2] you can get any type of kitchen or home gadget you could need at the fraction of the cost that you would spend at Chedraui. They aren't the most high-end products, but they are by far the cheapest.

Online Spanish Teacher: Cheapest & Best

Martin is my go-to guy. I was reluctant to share this because I selfishly don't want his schedule to fill up;

QR- 1 

QR- 2 

however, it's important to have some practice with this language in Tulum. You can get by just speaking English, but it's better to have at least some basics under your belt. You can practice with Martin before you come so you are prepared. His classes are between $5 USD and 7 USD depending on how you pay. Scan QR Code below[1] to message him on Whatsapp!

This might not be the first thing on your itinerary when visiting Tulum; however, for 90 USD, you can get three colon cleanses. These should be done about once a year. This is another way to support your health journey! Scan QR code[2] to cleanse that colon by sending Gabriela a WhatsApp Message!

QR- 1 

QR- 2 

Lashes & Brows: Cheapest & Best

I get my brows laminated, and then I get henna tattoos on them. I have never been happier with my brows! The price for this is around $30-$40 USD. I also get my lashes done here. A fill only costs $25 USD. She also does lash lifts, eyelash tinting, eyebrow tinting, & manicure/pedicure. I love supporting his woman and her son. She's amazing! Scan QR Code below[1] to send her a WhatsApp message.

Beach Hotels: Cheapest!

Okay, so as a local, I have never stayed at a hotel on the beach outside of Selina, where I lived for a year and three months. So, I've compiled a quick and clickable list for you to access if you want to stay on the beach for a discount.

Please note that these will still be expensive. It's not just expensive in Mexico. It's expensive in general. They will be way more expensive than staying in town. However,

QR- 1 

there is nothing quite like having the beach extra close. Please click the name of the hotel to access it.

- Zamas

- Rosa Del Viento

- Hotel Playa Xcanan Tulum

- La Posada del Sol Tulum

- Casa Ganesh

- Coco Tulum

- Selina: Please note that this is a shared kitchen/ shared spa.

Zamas	
Rosa Del Viento	
Hotel Playa Xcanan Tulum	
La Posada del Sol Tulum	
Casa Ganesh	
Coco Tulum	
Selina	

Chapter 5
WHERE TO IN TULUM

This Section will help you access my go-to places of whatever you could need in Tulum.

Water Delivery

Here you can access the mega jugs of drinking water below:

Jungle Rainwater: Scan QR Code below[1] to order on WhatsApp. The cost for your first bottle is 155 pesos, and you are paying for the plastic. Save the plastic to only pay for the water when you refill, which is 70 pesos.

Alkaline Water: Scan QR Code below[2] to order on WhatsApp. The cost of this water is 50

QR- 1 

QR- 2 

pesos for a refill and 150 pesos for the first bottle since you need to buy the plastic.

Cheapest Water: This water is about 36 pesos for a jug. Scan QR Code below[1] to order on WhatsApp.

Water Dispenser

You may need a water dispenser for these items, and you can access a cheap plastic version for 7 USD Scan QR Code below[2] or a more high-tech version in Walmart in Playa Del Carmen. See Chapter 7 to see how to access The Collectivo to Playa! Amazon also offers these.

QR- 1 

QR- 2 

Worried? Don't worry; Scan QR Code below[1] to get all the testing your heart desires. This can be a little pricey for a total scan, costing you about 2,400 pesos. Your travel insurance may cover it, so check with them. In the Inside Out Travelers Guide, you will have access to more info on how to get insurance!

Check out the Whatsapp list. Scan QR Code below[2] to access our document that has 34+ Whatsapp Chat groups for all of the different community groups and activities in Tulum!

Okay, so there is an abundance of places to get groceries,

QR- 1 

QR- 2 

and there are all different styles! So, I will explain all the different options to you below.

Chedraui: This is for those of you who love Walmart! This is the supercenter of Tulum. This is the biggest store we have and is also the most expensive. What's great is that you can get most things you need here, including housing supplies, food, name-brand products, clothing, body products, cleaning products, and more! The location of Chedraui is below[1].

Super AKI: This is the next biggest store. This is cheaper than Chedraui, and I like getting my healthy smoothie ingredients here. You will have less selection overall at this store, but you will still have many options! The location is below[2].

Pool/Local Grocery Spots: These are the little corner marts, and there is one that is a local favorite called Pool.

QR- 1 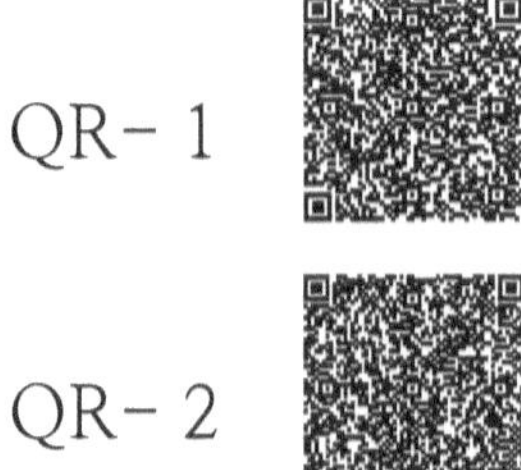

QR- 2

Scan QR Code below[1] to access this cheap, fresh, and healthy little mini

QR- 1

grocery spot. Below[1] is their second location! I love supporting these little establishments. You can also get bulk beans, quinoa, and oats here for cheap.

Bodega Aurora: This place is the cheapest grocery store. It's large and has your basic needs options. Scan QR Code below[2] to access it.

Health Food Grocery

There are healthy food options in Super Aki and Chedraui, and here are specialized food stores that I frequent below.

Gypsy Market: This is the most expensive grocery store, but it's AMAZING. Think mini Whole Foods. They

QR- 1 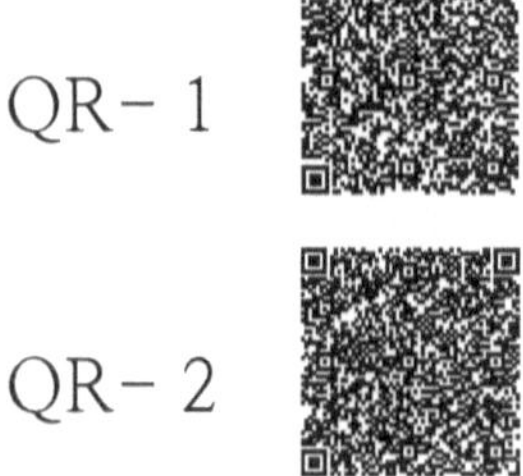

QR- 2

have all the best health and wellness options available to you! Scan QR Code below[1] to access.

Co.Con Amor: This has spices, vitamins, and other knickknacks to support your healthy lifestyle. Scan QR Code below[2] to access it.

QR- 1 

QR- 2

Woolis Foodie Market: This place has everything made from scratch and is delicious! Be sure to check out their Location BELOW[1]!

Recycling

Want to know where to recycle in Tulum? Here are the spots to check out: Tulum Circula: Scan QR Code below [2]to access. The recycling center is open 9–7 pm Mon thru Sat. They take cardboard, glass, plastic bottles, aluminum cans, tin cans, and electronics.

Composting

Woolis Foodie Market can be located Below[3] in town, or

QR- 1 

QR- 2

QR- 3

at the ladle community center, found Scan QR Code below[1].

You can donate clothing at Botanica Below[2]. Just message Fernando through QR CODE below[3] to organize! This clothing goes to underprivileged Mayan communities.

QR- 1 

QR- 2 

QR- 3

Fix A Broken Phone/Computer

Want to fix your computer? Anita and Fabians is your spot in Tulum. Scan QR Code below[1] to access

You can also go to the Mac store in Playa. Be warned; it will cost about $25 USD just for them to look at it. Apple products and most electronics are much more expensive in Mexico.

Botox, Fillers & Surgeries: The Best Surgeon At Mexico Prices

There is only one doctor that I will recommend for

QR- 1 

anything Botox and fillers. We work exclusively with him because he is simply the best in town. It's amazing because you can get these services at a fraction of the cost of what you will spend in most home countries. Message Ally to book by Scanning QR Code below[1]!

You can go to Costamed for any medical emergencies in Tulum. Scan QR Code below[2] to access the location. They are open 24 hours a day. They don't have a Whatsapp number that I know of, but you can just stop there to speak with them or call internationally. The number is available by clicking the link.

Okay, so I haven't been able to try EVERYWHERE in Tulum, and I won't put my stamp of approval on just

QR- 1 

QR- 2 

anything. So, this next guide will be incredibly helpful for you to access whatever your heart desires here in Tulum.

There are over 350+ places inside this additional guide. All have been recommended by women in The Tulum Girl Gang. Someone recommended these, so I trust them more than what you randomly find on the internet. This is just basic contact info; however, in Tulum, you can't find most of these things on Google, so this is one of the most helpful insider tips guides you can access! Categories in this list include the following:

Mechanic, Ayurveda, Coffee/ Cafes, Bikes, Breathwork, Car rental, cenotes, cleaning, Cleansing, Clothing, Cooking Classes, Covid Tests, Co-Working, Daycare/ ChildCare, Dentist, Doctors, Facials, Farm To Table Organic Restaurants, Farms, Fitness, Food Delivery, Gym, Hair Dressers, Hair Masks, Healing Therapy, Healthy Grocery Stores, Hypnosis, Lashes/Eyebrows, Laundry, Life Coach, LGBTQIA, Mani/Pedi, Massage, Natural Beauty & Hygiene, Organic Delivery Services, Organic Greens, Organic Local Brands, Organic Stores

In Tulum, Personal Trainers, Pet Food, Pet Sitters, Dog Boarding, Pet Spa, Photographer, Videographer, Pole dance, Realtor, Personal Meal Prep, Salsa, Scooter Rentals, Sound Bowl Healing, Spanish Teacher, Swimsuit, Taxi, Temazcal, Tulum Driver's License, Vet Volunteering, Waxing, Yacht Rental, & Yoga.

Scan QR Code below to access this document![1]

QR- 1 

Chapter 6
HELPFUL HACKS & INFO

How To Get A Mexican License As A Foreigner

R each out to Ally on WhatsApp by Scanning QR Code below[1]. It will cost about 1800 pesos and help you get local discounts in town. Also, having a

QR- 1

Mexican license, which you don't technically need by law, doesn't hurt when pulled over by a cop to show you are less of a tourist.

Okay, this was a life-changing hack when I first moved to Mexico. For about $2.50 USD, you can buy these plug-ins at Chedraui or Super Aki, and you will not be bothered at night. This allowed me to sleep in peace, knowing the mosquitoes would not attack me.

Itchy Bug Bit Relief

If you suffer from any itchy bug bites, run the bites under almost burning hot water to relieve the itchiness. This works 100% of the time. The water needs to be right under burning temperature. So, basically not too hot to handle, just a little under that. Let the water run on the bites for about 30 seconds, and you will feel instant relief.

You can also buy this life-changing tool on Amazon before you arrive, which is 1000%

better than any itch cream. Scan QR Code below[1] to access it.

QR– 1 

Bugs To Know In Tulum

You will encounter a handful of flying critters. None are life-threatening. Here are a few I've encountered:

- Mosquitos are a thing. Be sure always to have mosquito repellant and itch cream in your bag. Some places have more mosquitos than others.

- Tabanos are basically like horseflies. You can recognize them because they are colorful. The sting is really painful and will swell. Take some Advil, and the swelling will subside.

- Fleas are usually on the stray animals, so be wary. They are extra itchy and bite you around the feet, ankles, and lower legs.

Being aware of these bugs will allow you to protect yourself from them. They are not life-threatening.

Dealing With Parasites

So, getting a parasite is not uncommon in Mexico. It may be a parasite if you're feeling low energy, constant hunger, or any other weird health issues. Scan QR Code below[1] to learn a bit more about parasites.

Now, I bring this up to support you with a few resources in case you need to find out if you have one. I will also provide you with some resources to clear the parasite.

- Doctor Duparat: This doctor will perform a stool test to see if you have a parasite. If you do, this doctor will give you parasite medicine. He has holistic options and less holistic options, depending on the type of medicine you prefer. The cost is 150 USD for this service. With travel insurance, this should be covered.

QR- 1 

Scan QR Code below[1] to message him.

- **Kambo:** Kambo is a very holistic option to heal parasites. To learn more

about this option, Scan QR Code below[2]. I've worked with Indi for general cleanses with Kambo, and she's awesome!

QR- 1 

QR- 2 

- Parasite Tincture: For 200 pesos, you can access a parasite cleanse tincture. Scan QR Code below[1] to message the girl who sells it.

Since Tulum is pretty hot, you may experience mold. Here's how to spot it:

Mold on clothes can generally be identified by its smell. If you have a mold problem in your house, or specifically on your clothes, you will be able to identify it from its strong, musty, earthy odor. The appearance of the white and black mold is often easy to spot by the naked eye because of the discoloration it causes.

Are you regularly using a machine, hand wash, or dry cleaner to clean your clothes? For each technique, here is how to best remove mold.

Machine Wash:

QR– 1 

If the infestation isn't out of control, washing and drying the clothes might be enough. Most fungi species can be killed when exposed to water over 140-degrees Fahrenheit. Luckily, most machines include a "hot washing mode" reaching this temperature.

- Separate the infected clothes: As spores spread, don't mix moldy garments with clean ones.

- Select the hottest mode: Cold or

warm water won't affect mold. Ensure that the temperature won't damage the fabric.

- Pour detergent: You can use your regular laundry detergent.

- Wash: Let your machine run for two full cycles.

- Dry your clothes: The sun is a natural fungus killer. Hang your wet clothes outside under direct sunlight.

- Drier alternative: Transfer the clothes to your dryer immediately after the second cycle.

Warning

If the smell remains after washing, do not dry — spores are still present. Try soaking your clothes in vinegar or baking soda for 20 minutes and wash again.

Buy this at your local grocery store to avoid mold from growing in your closet!

Cell Phone Plans

Sims in Tulum: To get a SIM card, head to any Tel Cell locations to access a SIM card. Scan QR Code below[1] for one of the many locations.

Plans: If you don't speak Spanish, the easiest thing to do is re-up on the Recharge app since it's in English. You can get a SIM card for less than $10 USD, and your

QR- 1

plan every month can be as cheap as $10 USD. It's a great deal.

You can also get a monthly plan that I currently use for 25ish dollars instead of a Mexican number; you'll have your number from the states ported. Scan QR Code below[1] to access it. Please note that you will need to get the sim card from Amazon. It will be way cheaper to buy in the states on Amazon versus in Mexico.

Want food delivered right to you for some first-world comfort and luxury-style living? Check out www. Tomato.MX. It's is the place to have food delivered directly to your house! They let you know when it's being prepared, delivered, and on the way!

QR- 1 

Also, Chedraui is a grocery store that delivers. You can download the app to order. The app picture is orange with three humans pushing a cart. See the below image to know what to look for.

In Tulum, you can't drink the water. However, there are many companies you can use to make sure you are provided for. Below is a list of a few options!

So, scan QR code[1] to get a detailed article on water and food safety in Mexico. This blog does an incredible job

QR- 1 

at accurately sharing valuable information on how to avoid getting sick.

Hair Hack: Stop The Frizz And Save Your Curls

Okay, Tulum will take a beating on your hair. Now, I have curly, frizzy hair. This hack has worked wonders for girls with curly hair. I can't speak for straight-haired girls, but I can tell you that whether you are curly-haired or straight, don't wash your hair with shower water. I put a big jug of drinking water on a table in my shower, and I rinse my hair with that. You can also just put the water in a pitcher to pour on your head.

I put two tablespoons of vinegar and one liter of water mixed in a spray bottle.

I bought the spray bottle from the kitchen supplies store, which you can find under this book's cheapest and best section. I do shampoos only a few times a month to preserve the natural oils. If you are going to shampoo, wash with shampoo and conditioner, avoiding the shower water. Rinse, spray the vinegar solution on the hair, leave for five minutes, then wash with drinking water. Side note, it can be white or apple cider vinegar!

This has made such a difference in my hair. Many people, including myself, have struggled to keep our hair looking alive until we identified this solution.

Chapter 7
TRANSPORTATION OPTIONS

The cheapest way to the airport is to take the ADO bus for $15 one way. Direct buses from the airport to Tulum end around 9:00 p.m. If you get in later, you can take a bus to Playa and take another bus from Playa to Tulum. This is very easy as you don't even need to leave the bus station for the transfer. You will need to take a taxi from the ADO bus station in Tulum to your apartment.

You can also take a shuttle from Cancun Airport to Tulum for about $25–$30.

Taxi is fairly expensive, ranging from $60–$85 one way. This will give you door-to-door service. You can access safe taxi cabs with this resource guide. Scan QR Code below[1] to access it.

QR– 1 

Finally, you can use these groups to access ride shares to and from Tulum. Scan QR Code below[1] to access the WhatsApp links to access the groups!

ADO BUS

This will take you all over Mexico for really affordable prices. You can book bus tickets by Scanning QR Code below[2].

The Collectivo Van In Tulum

So, the first and cheapest option is taking The Collectivo. This is a van.

Times: This van runs from about 8:00 a.m.to 8 p.m., maybe 9:00 p.m. if you're lucky.

Cost: This van is incredibly cheap. The cost was 20 pesos which are about $1 USD, to take you to and from town.

QR– 1 

QR– 2 

Pickup Locations: Now, the downside is that you can wait quite a while. You may have to walk 10 minutes or more to get to a Collectivo station in town. This bus will stop for you when riding to town on the beach strip just about anywhere, so getting to town is easy. There are only a few stops in town to get the collective to the beach. Scan QR Code below[1] to access the first bus

QR- 1 

stop location for the beach. It also stops at Chedraui, which is HERE[1].

My biggest issue with taking this van is that it can get packed. There were about 12 people in this tiny van on my way to town, and that was way too much closeness for me. I loved the price, however!

QR– 1 

Use this super cheap hack! You can take the Collectivo to Playa for only 50 pesos ($2.50 USD)! Pick up is at the 7-Eleven diagonal from Super Aki in Tulum, or you can also go diagonal from ADO bus station in Tulum. I prefer by 7-Eleven to skip Tulum town traffic.

They leave every 5 minutes and drop you off at Chedraui in Playa Del Carmen. They can also drop you off at the plaza near Sam's Club. This is the cheapest, fastest, and easiest way to get to Playa.

The parking lot is about a block behind the main road when you want to leave Playa. (Drop off and pick up locations are different). Scan QR Code below[1] to access the location for pick up in Playa.

Now, lots of people enjoy this mode of transportation. You can rent or buy a bike. You can easily buy a bike in

QR- 1 

Playa Del Carmen at a Walmart for 2400 pesos ($106 USD) to 5000 pesos ($222 USD). You will want to either rent a car to get it or just confirm the bus will be able to bring the bike back before doing this.

You can also buy a bicycle on the Facebook marketplace, which has all sorts of offers. This is the route I would take to save yourself the time and hassle. I saw bikes as low as 500 pesos which is $22 USD. Just repost it online for the next person to buy from you when you're finished!

Downsides To A Bicycle In Tulum:

The downside to this is that in the summer months, it is HOT. Riding the bike between 9:00 a.m. and 6:00 p.m., you will sweat. If you sweat a lot in general, you may also sweat in the winter months.

Feeling just how hot it was without being on a bike made it clear that I was not okay with sweating profusely on my way to anywhere I was going.

The other issue is that if you want to go to town from

the beach or vice versa, it's still pretty far by bike. You are looking at about 30-45 minutes or more.

Also, I feel that riding a bike in the dark is not safe. There is not much light on the many roads, and a bicycle would be an easy target if someone did feel like robbing you on your way home. So, for these reasons, I chose not to buy a bicycle.

The other option is to rent a bicycle. You can rent one for $5 USD a day outside the Selina hotel.

___

Now, this is the most expensive option. To get to and from town, the cost is 200 pesos to 300 pesos. In USD,

that's about \$10 USD to \$15 USD. The price from town to the beach can be a lot more. It ranges from 300 pesos to 800 pesos depending on the time of year and driver. I always avoid this since this is, by far, one of the biggest rip-offs in Tulum. If you want to order a taxi, use the above guide or Scan QR Code below[1]!

QR- 1 

Renting A Scooter

This is a great option to make sure you have mobility around town, and in Tulum, you need it. The benefit of this is that you will easily have no worries about registration, securing the bike, and not having to find someone to sell your bike to at the end.

Most scooters in town go for at least 25 USD to 60 USD a day. Want a Deal?

Scan QR Code below[1] to Whatsapp message Ally, who rents scooters. They have one of the best reputations.

Mention that you read about them in this book, and you can rent a scooter for anywhere from $17 to $30 a day, depending on the season. You can buy a scooter; however, if you want to be hassle-free and not deal with the chaos of buying one, this is the best spot to rent.

QR- 1 

Renting A Car

So, for this option, I would recommend getting a car at the airport. Renting cars can be fairly expensive in Tulum. The way to get the best deal is to go to each counter and let them know you are pricing out each place to ensure they give you their best rate. While I think scooters are better, cars have their perks. They have AC, they are safer, and it's great when you go grocery shopping.

As far as places in Tulum, check Jose. Scan QR Code below[1] to Whatsapp him! Prices in Tulum can change based on the season, but in October, he was charging $30 a day with half coverage and $50 a day for full coverage for a medium-sized vehicle. For their small cars, they were charging $20 USD a day.

QR- 1 

Chapter 8

BUYING NEW AND USED SCOOTERS

Buying a scooter is a great option because it is a cost-friendly way to get around town. While this is the cheapest option, it is the most challenging to maneuver.

However, with the right information, you can do it

smoothly. I spent a ton of time researching and asking questions and found the following info.

Buying A New Scooter As An Expat

You can't buy a Moto at every location as an ex-pat. In some places, you need to be a local. The two places you can visit to buy as an ex-pat are Italika on the main road located HERE[1] and the second place is Chedraui which is located HERE[2].

You can also go to Playa, where you may be able to find a few deals!

Registering A New Scooter

Okay, so registering a scooter can be as easy

QR- 1 

QR- 2 

as you want it to be. Things that are easy in your home country can be challenging in Tulum. So, if you decide you want to buy a scooter, a few hacks will support you in this process.

The easiest, but most expensive way to get any scooter registered is by reaching out to Ally. See below under registering without the appropriate paperwork.

The second easiest option is buying new. This is the easiest way to register a scooter. You will need the following:

- Passport
- Copy of Passport
- License
- Copy of License
- Apt Lease or Rental Agreement
- Copy of Apt Lease or Rental Agreement
- Factura (Invoice)
- Copy of Factura

You make an appointment by Scanning QR Code below[1] and need a CURP number to register for an appointment. If you don't have a CURP number, ask a Mexican friend to make you an appointment. Or you can message by Scanning QR Code below[2] to have someone make an appointment The cost is $20 USD.

The location is located behind the grocery store called Aurora Bodega. You can find it where the blue dot on the map below is.

QR– 1 

QR– 2 

109
eurodental
odontología
a Fonda Tulum
VILLAS
Super Aki Tulum
Vegan Tulum
307
Juice Lover
15
CrissPac
COL HURACANES
500 ft
200 m
Google

Get A Moto Registered Without Appropriate Papers

The easiest but most expensive way to get any scooter registered (used or new) is by reaching out to Ally. You can buy almost anything in Tulum if you're willing to pay, including your moto being registered. This is great if you don't have a CURP number to make an appointment at the DMV of Mexico or if you don't have the correct paperwork for a used Moto.

You can be missing all of the paperwork and still get the

bike registered. Message Ally on Whatsapp by Scanning QR Code below[1]. This will cost between $175 and $300 USD in total. This can be for new and used bikes.

So, I bought a scooter used. This was the route that seemed to make the most sense. However, after buying it, I learned I didn't have all the appropriate paperwork to register it. Trying to get it registered alone was a nightmare. So, I ended up paying $250 USD to have it done behind the scenes. From an ease-of-use standpoint, I recommend a new scooter. If you're on a budget, a used scooter will do.

I went on Facebook Marketplace, and there were many different options to choose from for buying. I bought a 2020 Italika scooter with 500km on it. Italika has been a good brand for a short period. The bike brand is manufactured in China. So, while it's not great quality

QR- 1 

for the long term, it's fine for a bit of time. The quality brands include Kawasaki, Honda, and Yamaha. Italika parts are cheap to repair in town, which is a perk of this brand.

Try to find a scooter already registered with plates that don't have too many miles or damage. Register the Moto with the person you buy it from at the Tulum DMV. Look for newer scooters. New ones pop up every day on the marketplace.

Registering A Used Moto

Make sure the license plate and registration are up to date when driving. Find out when the bike will need to be registered again. You can use the bike if it is registered to someone else.

If you got pulled over by the Mexican police, you just say you are using the bike of a friend. Bikes need to be registered yearly. The Tulum DMV can give you a complete checklist of anything you need when purchasing a used bike.

Now, buying a used bike can be dangerous because it's a second-hand market you're buying from. Bring someone with you when buying the bike to minimize the risk involved. See the bike first and go without a bunch of valuables or money on you.

Do the bike and money transfers during the day and in a populated area. Inside a bank is a

great place to exchange money and key/paperwork where there is security. If you can, skip the cash and try to do an electric money transfer in person.

Also, if you do not speak Spanish, it's best to bring a friend who does if your seller does not have English-speaking skills.

Visit the Government Location for Vehicle Transfers. If you want to get additional information to fact-check to get an official opinion, you can go to the local office to confirm all is good with the bike you will be purchasing. You can get the plate numbers and check that the bike is in good standing. This place is located in Andador Plaza behind Bodega Aurrera.

Selling Your Bike

A word of advice: If you register the bike in your name, it's not a good idea to give it away with your registration and plates. Technically, if something happens, you are liable. While many people do this practice when selling a bike, it is advised against for your protection.

You will need to follow the exact process with your buyer as you did as a buyer but from the seller's side.

If you want to sell your bike and the bike is in your name, please see the list of paperwork items needed to buy so you can educate your buyer and prepare them for success when they buy from you.

Chapter 9

DRIVING IN TULUM TIPS

Insurance is optional, but you should consider getting it. I do not have insurance yet, but I will update you on the process once I do. You will need the original factura (invoice) to get insurance.

Do I Need A Special License To Drive?

As long as you have a license, you should be good to go. You don't need any special permits.

Do I Need A Helmet?

Yes, you need a helmet on a scooter. The police can be strict. Don't test the waters. You can get a scooter helmet for about 300 pesos ($15 USD) from a scooter repair shop in the town. Ask locals if you need help locating these places. I found mine on Satelite Street. Save yourself a ticket and maybe even your life. Get a helmet.

Where To Buy Cheap Helmets In Town

You can buy a helmet for your scooter at this local store

by Scanning QR Code below[1]. They have all different types, with their cheapest helmet being $15 USD.

Scooter theft is a major issue in Tulum, and there are tools you can come prepared with to keep your scooters and not get them stolen or towed!

Here are a few important tips that will save you thousands of dollars:

Buy an apple AirTag. Scan QR Code below[2] to view. You can buy it at the Apple store in Playa Del Carmen for about $35–$40 USD or online before you leave the states for about $30 USD. You can tape it to your scooter. Make sure to buy extra quality duct tape because the heat can make it peel. The best bet is to use duct tape and dab it with gorilla glue so it doesn't peel off. Make sure to hide in an unnoticeable place and in a spot that

QR– 1 

QR– 2 

won't get lost if it falls out. So, it's best to tape inside the scooter.

Buy a bike lock and place it around the back tire. It's even better to lock the bike to something.

Always lock the front wheel. Turn the wheel to the left and turn the key to the left to lock the steering wheel and front tire.

Avoid Getting Towed In Tulum!

To prevent towing, always check to make sure there isn't a sign with an "E" that has a slash through it. If you are an English speaker, you are used to seeing a P; however, in Spanish, Parking is "estacionamiento."

 The beach road is a tow haven, so never

park on the beach road. Always stick to parking in the restaurants.

Okay, so the first step is going to the police station, which is located near Chedraui The location is HERE[1]. You will pay about 800 pesos here just for the paperwork. You will need cash.

Then, you will need to get a taxi or plan to walk about an hour (have cash for the taxi) to pick up your scooter at the tow station. The location is HERE[2].

For scooters, it's about 3,000 pesos ($150 USD), and for a car, it's about 5,000 pesos ($250 USD). Make sure to have cash for this activity. Sometimes they accept credit cards, and sometimes they don't. Plan to pay a fee for using the credit card, so cash is always better.

QR- 1 

QR- 2 

Gas Hack: Don't Get Scammed

Okay, always keep your eye out at the gas stations. I've heard of people being charged double or triple because they were not paying attention. Make sure the gas counter starts at zero. For a scooter, the amount should be around 100 pesos.

Handling the Police When Pulled Over In Tulum

You don't usually have to worry about

getting pulled over in town. On the beach road, there are occasional checkpoints. I don't make eye contact at checkpoints and always just keep driving. They will never chase you if you don't stop. They are checking for passports. No Alcohol, no license, not speeding, etc.

Special Hack: I do my best never to make eye contact at checkpoints to avoid getting pulled over. I keep driving forward and pretend like I don't see anything happening. If they wave at me, I keep driving. I only stopped once because they shouted, and I was on a dirt road while turning, so I didn't have much choice.

Hack 2: When on a scooter, I drive past the

cop when a car passes simultaneously. So, the car is essentially between my scooter and the cop.

- If you get pulled over, only if they ask, say you are borrowing a friend's bike. If they ask you for money, ask to speak to a supervisor. If they say no, ask them to take you to the office. They will let you go. They prey on easy tourists. They don't want to do the paperwork, and it's illegal for them to ask for money.

- The way they force you to pay them on the spot is by holding your license. They tell you that they won't

give it back. A great hack that will help you is to get a copy of your license and passport, then laminate them. It will only cost a few dollars. You can Scan QR Code below[1] to access the location. Then, you had over the laminated copy so if they won't give it back; you can tell them to keep it.

Important Details when riding:

- Always carry your license and a copy of your passport.

- Always lock the bike steering wheel at night and try to secure the bike to something with the bike lock.

- Do not park on the main beach road. You will likely get towed. Be sure to always park at the restaurants.

QR– 1 

- Make sure to go SLOW on bumpy dirt roads and over-speed bumps. They can cause external damage to the bike.

Ok, so want to carry more things on your scooter without putting yourself in danger? Head to your local hardware store and buy the plastic zip pull ties for about one dollar. Scan QR Code below[1] to see an example.

Then, go to Chedraui and ask the veggie section for an extra basket (these are the baskets the veggies are stored in). They have them available and will give you one for free. Ziplock the basket/crate onto the back of your bike for a crate that will help you carry more when on a scooter!

QR- 1 

Chapter 10

STAYING LONG TERM

Can I Have A Bank Account In Tulum?

As a foreigner on a tourist visa, you cannot get a bank account. As soon as you set up getting your temporary or permanent visa, you will be able to get a bank account.

Open A Bank Account As A Foreigner

As a foreigner (assuming you are not Mexican), you'll

need all these to open a Mexican bank account. Finding a bank was challenging because there were all sorts of options or weird different things you needed. Skip looking at BBVA & HSBC because they require an RFE number which you can only get in Playa. I found a simpler process with Santander. I had to have these to open there:

- Citizenship or residency visa

- Passport

- CURP number

- Print out of utility bill with your address. The bill doesn't have to be in your name, but it can't be a companys name.

- Lease Agreement

- Mexico phone number (I used a friend's phone number for a while, but you do need to be able to access this because they text you with access codes to set up online banking). You can reference getting a Mexican SIM Card section to set up a Mexican bank account.

- Beneficiary name and DOB

- **Two personal references:** You'll need their names, an address in Tulum along with a Mexican phone number. I guess this is to make sure you're not a serial killer or a bank robber.

Visa Types In Mexico

So, there are six types of Visas to know about. I did the 4-year temporary VISA process, which I will explain more about. Just to give you a general idea of the types, see the list below:

• Family Visa– For if you get married and have a child.

• Money Visa– Economic Solvency; this means you have lots of money

• Retired Visa– This is for anyone retired.

• Job Visa– Create a company and put it as a shareholder; the same company issues a job offer and needs $3k each month for the last 12 months. You need to fly to Florida for this.

• Four years of temporary Visas with an expired visa (this is what I recommend and explain below)

• Tourist Visa– Costs nothing, can get up to 6 months, but six months is not guaranteed.

Get A 4-Year Temp Visa

If you visited Mexico in 2020 or before and have an expired tourist VISA, you are eligible for this program. For about 22,000 pesos ($1,100 USD), you can have a lawyer get this set up for you.

You would visit Merida the day before your Visa expires, and the lawyer would walk you through the process. Scan QR Code below[1] to get linked up with the lawyer I

QR- 1

used and who I very much trust. This is one of the most simple and cheap ways to get your Visa.

Be sure to talk to your accountant about the FEIE Credit that allows you not to pay federal and state taxes on the first 108k of your earnings. This could save you 10k+ in tax money to the government. After speaking with CPAs in Mexico, you won't pay Mexican taxes if you work online and don't have a business in Mexico! Scan QR Code below [1] for more info!

QR– 1 

Renting An Apartment

Want to come to Tulum and stay for a while? Well, there are some important tips to know. First, please understand the prices will change based on the season. Summer time is the cheapest, and wintertime is the most expensive. I will provide you with some resources and tips on handling this task.

The best places to look for apartments are in Facebook groups, on the Facebook marketplace, real estate group chats, and Airbnb.

Airbnb

If you are going to look on Airbnb and stay longer than a few weeks, it's best to rent a place for a few days, and then when you get here, inquire about a place you are interested in on Airbnb and request to go see it. Then when you get there, you can negotiate with them. Lots of places will work with you. The only time this may be challenging is during the high season. During low season, everyone has lots of vacancies, so there will be plenty of room for negotiation.

Facebook Groups

You can utilize our Facebook groups doc that has an organized list of all Facebook Tulum groups. There is a section to post on and see other postings specifically for real estate, but don't limit yourself just to the real estate groups. Post in all the groups and share what you are looking for. You can also click the search icon in the Facebook groups and type in "rentals" to see who has recently posted about rentals. Make sure to toggle "recent." Scan QR Code below[1] to access our Facebook groups list!

Facebook Market Place

This will have the most organized set-up and best deals. Often, this is for longer-term rentals. Tulum will give cheaper pricing for longer stays. Always try to negotiate

QR- 1 

on the price. You can sometimes get a discount by offering to pay a few months up-front.

Important Questions to ask and things to consider:

1.   Cost of the AC bill on average: Some places have higher bills than others. It could be an error they are experiencing with the electric company, it could be the type of ACs they have, it could be that the apartment has a history of higher usage or seen as a rental property, which sometimes they charge more for. So always ask to see a copy of the bill.

2. Always ask the current or most recent tenants to speak with a reference. This is Mexico. There are lots of pretend "nice" places. They may look good on the outside, but they have some hidden issues that you would only find out by living there.

3. Make sure to do a walk-through with the person renting the place. Count every item (sheets, things in

the kitchen, etc.), and take a photo of every issue or damage. There are lots of landlords who don't play nice. They will take your security deposit without thinking twice.

4. Confirm with the landlord that they have zero intention of renting in high season and are not allowed to kick you out during that season. Yes, this is a thing. Places can make a LOT of money by renting in December, Jan, Feb, and March. I've seen lots of people get booted from their places and then forced into a tough situation because the cost of renting at that time was so high.

5. Ask if there is noise or construction. Ask for a clause to leave the lease if there is construction noise that starts. Tulum is in a building phase so it's a must-ask question. Otherwise, you might drive yourself crazy from the noise.

6 . Ask about 24/7 security. I will not rent unless this

is present. A security system can work, but I would not rent unless there is a human that guards the place.

7. What are the roads leading to the apartment? Not all roads are paved, and it is a buzz kill to ride a road that has giant potholes in it. I recommend renting a place with a paved road and some lighting.

These are just a few under-the-radar things to think about when choosing a place!

Conclusion

Tulum is a magical place that people fall in love with. This guide will help you to navigate the challenges that can be tough in Tulum. I hope you found this helpful. If you found any errors in this book or things that were not accurate, please message Ally at +15182299283. I hope you fall in love with Tulum the way I have. I hope you have a smooth experience and experience this place's beauty.

Scan QR Code below[1] to access all our click-able resources from the guide in one spot.

QR- 1 

Thank
You